Economic Rents, the Hidden Profit

ECONOMIC RENTS, THE HIDDEN PROFIT

HOW TO IDENTIFY SAFE COMPANIES TO INVEST IN

BY

TIM WALSHAW

ISBN: 978-0-9874946-9-6

Previous related publication by Tim Walshaw:
Increasing Returns to Scale: *A Simple Way to Make Good Investments, and Not Bad Investments, When Investing in Company Shares*. **Published 2014.**

<publisher Tim Walshaw>
<Canberra, Australia>

<2015

Contents

Preface

Before I start on the subject of this short book, I believe it is necessary to say just a little about myself, and why I came to write this book.

I am a university graduate in economics and an economist by trade. And by trade, I mean a very practical economist, who through his professional lifetime has used his knowledge to advance the economic welfare (all right, wealth, but economist love using these high sounding terms) of first his employers and then his clients. I started my professional life as an economist in a government economic research organization, but I found that a government research organization was an oxymoron, and went out on my own. I started in international consultancy, and then followed the money trail to investment and financial advice, and prospered.

Why did I prosper? I used my knowledge of economics, and economic theory, to vastly improve the quality of investment advice. Most investment advice is bad, and loses clients money. I began by providing macro advice, that is advice on the outlook of the economy, and I was better than 8 out of 10 economists proffering this advice. But I moved into microeconomic advice, that is advice on individual firms; how they were structured, how they performed. And yes, my advice was vastly better and more profitable than advice given by other company analysts.

Why? Not because I claim to be cleverer, though I admit that in the vast majority of cases I was. No, it was because the current investment advice methodology is fundamentally flawed. It falls into two categories, "stories", (including the illegal insider sort), and "accounting ratios".

You have all seen investment 'stories'. Your stockbroker sends them incessantly. If you are a fund manager you get a stack of them every day, often from your own inside analysts. "Such and such a mine has found a new deposit. Such a company has been given a big contract. The economy is picking up, and consumers like x company cars." If you rush out and buy (or occasionally sell) on the basis of these stories, and if the stories always work, you would be a millionaire in no time at all. Older and wiser investors know that the vast majority of these stories fall flat. They never seem to resolve into higher long-term profits. I call these stories 'tips', and they are less valuable than on the racetrack. At least on the track there are only a small number of horses in each race. On the stock market there are myriads of share issues.

Accounting ratios. They often come with the stories. It is an attempt to appear 'scientific'. The liquidity ratio is such and such, and the quick ratio is such and such. Accountants (there are too many of them in investment) have taken over the investment advice industry, and they use these ratios non-stop. Yes, these ratios can often be useful, especially if a company is in a bad way. Most companies attempt to keep their ratios in acceptable bounds. If they are unable to do this, this is an obvious sign that the company is in trouble. Ratio analysis can prevent you making a bad investment, and thus losing your money. But making more money? I have yet to see any example where investing in a company with 'good' ratios makes money. "They have a good liquidity ratio, therefore I must invest." Warren Buffett claims to do this, but I am pretty sure his investigations go much deeper than that.

Furthermore, from an economic point of view, averages and ratios are nonsense, as everything happens at the 'margin'. But marginal analysis is difficult, usually requiring economic models, expertise and the use of computers. Even if most investment analysts knew how to do marginal analysis, most investors would not understand the result. The method I propose is a simplified method of marginal analysis, and yes, it uses a simplified economic model.

Yes, I do have issues with accountants and accounting rules. Briefly because you cannot trust the published profits, among a lot of other things. Between double entry bookkeeping and the published figures a lot of nasty things happen. For instance, profit figures are adjusted upwards in the accounting process by increases in capital values. Also in my opinion accrual accounting is a recipe for deceit, as used by Enron. As an economist I take strong exception to this activity. For my clients, I calculate the 'real' profits, the "economic rents" of a company. I have a nifty way of doing this, as will be shown later in this book.

This book is about a quick, easy and highly effective method of finding the true state of a company. How prosperous it is in terms of its income. This method finds the "hidden profits" of a company. What its real profits in relation to its income and assets used to make these profits. What is the "margin of safety" and the likelihood of things going bad. What is the likelihood they are going to make good profits next year.

So what is this measure? The economic term is ECONOMIC RENTS (often loosely called monopoly rents – though in actual fact there are very few monopolies as such.) The aim is to invest in companies with HIGH ECONOMIC RENTS, and avoid companies with LOW ECONOMIC RENTS. These economic rents will be compared between companies using a meaningful ratio.

Introduction

Investors have two purposes for investing their money. Making more money, whether from income or capital gains; and not losing it. It would be ideal if you could do both, but in the vast majority of cases making more money carries an element of risk that you could lose money. There are many investors, a sizable proportion, who wish to invest with the minimum of risk, even though sometimes this reduces the return on that investment.

The obvious choice for the latter type of investor are Government Bonds, which supposedly carry minimal risk. In actual fact such an assumption of minimal risk for Government Bonds is untrue. Recent events show that Bonds of many countries are certainly not risk free, carrying with them at least a high inflation rate eroding your capital, or even a likelihood of default. Yes, even the Bonds issued by the United States Government may lose money from time to time, if not directly from default, but from increases in interest rates, or even deliberately engineered inflation!

It may be heretical to say this, but stocks and shares issued by certain well-run companies carry less risk and greater return than many, if not most, government bonds. And the assets of many of these companies, if they are international in scope, are often beyond the remit of the "home" government.

What are these companies? Is there a logical way of identifying them? And indeed, is this type of companies large and monopolistic? Are there smaller companies that can be identified by the proposed method that are equally a good investment and nearly as safe (though more dependent on the relevant home government not going off the rails)?

The answer to these questions is – yes, there is. Furthermore, there is a quick and easy method to identify these companies.

What is it? Economic rents. There is a quick and easy method to calculate the economic or monopoly rent for any company. An "economic rent" is not an accounting profit. There is in actual fact very little connection between the size of profits calculated by accountants and the size of economic rents. In fact, for those companies with high economic rents, the economic rent is often well hidden and the accounting profits tend to underestimate its value.

And surprise, surprise, those companies with low economic rents often record high accounting profits. There is little or no correlation between low or high accounting profits and the size of economic rents.

Why invest in companies with high economic rents? SAFETY. These companies have a high proportion of "economic fat" in their income. These companies can be heavily squeezed before they begin to make a loss. You can safely invest in these companies, knowing that in bad times profits will not fall much. Current dividends are likely to be continued to be paid without putting any strain on the company, or incurring borrowing.

These companies are also a GOOD INVESTMENT. In order to reap high economic rents they these companies must be well run; and often be in an industry that facilitates the achievement of high economic rents, through being a quasi monopoly, or having its product in strong demand, or benefiting from some technological advantage.

However there is a caveat. There is one industry that almost automatically imparts high economic rents – banking. While all banks do not automatically have high economic rents, this outcome is more likely than not for banks, especially among the larger banks. However, because banks are highly leveraged they are a lot more risky. Also from my long study of the banking industry, in my opinion the honesty of senior banking employees are often not of the highest. As a result the inherent risk of the banking industry is much higher than for other industries, even for the next most risky activity, mining. Therefore as I will describe later in this book, I recommend under-weighting banks in your portfolio if the main purpose of your investment strategy is to reduce risk.

However do not just assume any and every bank has a high economic rent. I stress in this book that the situation for EVERY company must be individually estimated for their financial results.

Do companies with high economic rents exist? Yes, they are many of them. They need not be large nor well known, nor blatant monopolists, nor their profits maintained by government action. Many medium sized companies, even small ones, incur high economic rents. The purpose of this book is to help you identify them.

Sometimes these high economic rent companies do not have high reported asset reserves (the result of previous high economic rents), - they keep them well hidden – nor do they have high dividend payouts. But the only way to estimate the level of economic rents is described in this book. The accounting ratios commonly used for investment purposes to try to identify monopoly rents, such as asset ratios, are often nonsense.

What characterizes a company with high economic rents? They make high gross profits year after year, with little apparent effort. They often can't help making money. You get the impression that the management just do what they do, and somehow they sit on a pile of cash, and any borrowing is purely voluntary and for tax purposes.

Yes, the shares of many of these companies keep increasing in price. You suspect the companies are sitting on rivers of gold, and the management knocks off at three to play golf.

So the purpose of this book is to identify companies with HIGH ECONOMIC RENTS, related to some suitable factor as a ratio, and set up a methodology to invest in these company shares. This book also describes a method to invest with an optimal distribution of shares in a portfolio.

But WHY am I writing this book? To make a few dollars selling it? No. In the hope of gaining commissions for economic advice? No. After reading this book, you can do the investment yourself. You don't need my advice. Anyway, I don't need these commissions.

The reason I am writing this book is to improve the world.

Yes, if enough investors use this technique, analyzing company financial company statements to find the size of their economic rents will be become a standard procedure. All investors will benefit. No company will be able to hide the size of their economic rent, big or small.

Chapter 1

Definition of Economic Rents

What are Economic Rents? Economic Rents are also called Monopoly Profits, though that is not a complete description. While most non-economists instantly recognize what a Monopoly Profit is, and all Monopoly Profits are Economic Rents, there are many more examples of Economic Rents than there are of Monopoly Profits. Many Economic Rents are completely hidden, and have to be ferreted out, to your profit.

Throughout this book, the term Economic Rent will be used. It is a confusing term because it has little do with house rents or office rents per se. The term Rent is purely historic, and dates back to the writings of an early nineteenth century economist - David Ricardo. Ricardo was investigating the role of land rents and the influence they had on wheat prices, and showed that increasing land rents did not increase corn (wheat) prices. If a landowner increased his rents, the farmer could not increase the price of corn by "passing on" the rent increase. In the long term, as many 'squeezed' farmers got out, the only option for the landowner was to reduce his rents to allow the farmer to have a 'normal' profit. (David Ricardo 1817)

If on the other hand when wheat prices increased, landowners could grab the entire increase in profit, leaving the farmer with just his normal profit. This is the situation that Henry George railed against in the late 19th century. The owner of the land, whether rural or urban, obtained the entire economic rent due to increased income, whether or not he had worked for it. Henry George went further and identified economic rents on both urban and rural land as the ultimate cause of poverty. All the workers' economic rents due to any increase in productivity were extracted for the ultimate benefit of the landowner, reducing the worker back to poverty. (Henry George 1879).

While as an economist I would like to wax lyrical on the role of economic rents on income and prices, I shall refer you to other publications such as that by Henry George to learn about the very important effects they have on society and the economy. This book has a restricted aim – how to make money, and not lose money from a knowledge of economic rents.

Definition. **Economic Rents** are the "return over and above opportunity costs or the normal return necessary to keep a resource in its current use". (Morton, John S, Rae Jean B. Goodman (2003), cited by Wikipedia). For our purposes this is one of the most useful definitions, one of scores of definitions cited by Wikipedia, as it ascribes "normal return", and opportunity cost as part of the definition.

Normal returns or normal profits are the minimum level of profits caused by competition which allow a business to stay in business. In a competitive friction free economy, with no market failures, all business will operate under the same rate of profit, the normal profit. If any part of the economy has a higher rate of profit, competition will cause resources to shift to that part of the economy.

Opportunity cost is the value of the best alternative activity foregone in a situation in which choice need to be made between several mutually exclusive alternatives given limited resources.

As you will immediately deduce, in the real world, above normal returns can and do occur, and continue to persist. In a real world economy, frictions and market failures are endemic, and cause firms to have a persistently high rate of profit, and indeed a persistently low rate of profit, which would cause firms eventually to exit from that industry.

One cause, but not the only cause, of persistently high and above normal profits is risk. Yes, it is often the case, companies and industries which have higher risks also exhibit high economic rents. The market seems to create this situation, though this is not invariably the case. Since the purpose of this book is to demonstrate how to obtain a high economic rent in a low risk manner, the issue of risk has to be considered. There will be a chapter in this book on a methodology on how to modify your portfolio for risk. Not just removing "risky" companies, but concentrating your investment on high economic rent but low risk companies.

I shall confine most of this book to its main purpose – making money from a knowledge of how to estimate the Economic Rents of a quoted company. These figures are hidden, usually deliberately so, but if you ferret out the value of economic rents many companies are making, you stand to make a decent investment.

In my previous book, "Increasing Returns to Scale", I mentioned that I would write something on making money using the Cash Flow accounts published annually by every quoted company. The fundamental difference between increasing returns to scale and economic rents investment methodologies is that while the "Increasing Returns to Scale" methodology is dynamic – you are investing to make a return on increasing share prices, the "Economic Rent" methodology is essentially static. You are looking for companies with a lot of fat through the operation of hidden profits, in whose shares you intend to park chunks of money safely for the long term. You are not expecting significant share price increases unless these hidden rents are discovered by other investors.

The word for investing in economic rents is safety. A company with high economic rents is not likely to go bust in the immediate future. It does not need to be regularly checked upon. Just once a year check if the high rents are still there, and you can forget about this company investment for a year. The share price might not rise, but it is unlikely to fall much, even at the bottom of a share crash or recession.

It is common nowadays for certain investment commentators to describe investing in certain companies as investing in the "new government bonds". This is a reflection of the decline in credit worthiness of governments as well as the current (2014) low government interest rates. Yes, certainly, there are companies that are "safe" to invest in, and a very good way to identify this type of company is to identify and measure their economic rents. On the other hand just investing in a large company, a so-called "blue chip", is not necessarily a safe investment. I need only mention General Motors and General Electric (which have low economic rents).

Do high economic rent companies have high dividends? No, not necessarily so. In fact in my experience less than a third pay high dividends. But they accumulate and accumulate, in many cases while not working very hard. These are ideal 'set and forget' investments.

While saying this, I must warn that there is no such thing in reality as 'set and forget'. **The company annual accounts must be checked once a year at the time they are published to see if the economic rents are falling. This is very important.** Neglect this activity at your peril. There will be a chapter later on about this process.

Finally, you sometimes do get considerable capital gains from investing by using this methodology. Why? Take-overs. There are take-over merchants, whatever you like to call them, out there with large staffs chewing through published accounts looking just for this set up – companies with accumulated economic rents. They pounce, offer a price for which you can't say no, take over the company, strip it or whatever, gee up the management, and sell it a couple of years later at a substantial profit. If you have a high number of 'high economic rents' companies in your portfolio, on the law of averages you can make good profits in this manner.

The rest of this book goes through the theory of how to estimate the economic rents of a company, (the process is very simple – indeed one client managed to automate the process directly from data supplied electronically by a financial data aggregator), provides advice on choosing the best companies to invest in among the amazing plethora of companies you will find with high economic rents; and as in my last book on "Increasing Returns to Scale" a description of an optimal portfolio.

The methodology described in this book is relatively low effort, but many investors are happy with the results. Some claim that if you factor in take-overs, the capital gains are comparable to using the Increasing Returns to Scale methodology. I make clear that I make no such claims, and as you see from my disclaimer in the legal page, no guarantees of profits at all. I stress that in most cases, while this type of investment is safe, share prices won't rise by much, barring take-overs. But they won't usually fall by much either.

However your success in choosing the shares to invest in is entirely due to your own efforts in applying correctly the methodology as described in this book. But as I said previously, that won't be hard to do.

Chapter 2

How to Calculate Economic Rents

While for over a century the concept of economic rents had important theoretical implications, measuring its actual value remained elusive. Then along came E. Cary Brown. Once in a while a totally obscure economics professor comes up with something earth-changing, a single written article, and he then falls back to obscurity. Sometimes they keep up the good work, such as Ronald Coase; but in the case of E Cary Brown he made no further major discoveries in the study of economics.

What did E Cary Brown do? In an obscure article, part of a compendium of articles in an obscure book, written to celebrate the life of another economist, E Cary Brown (1948) described a methodology to calculate the economic rent earned by a firm. Not the accounting profit, which everybody knows covers a multitude of sins. Every economist involved in providing investment advice knows accounting profits provide information varying between useless to downright deceiving. (Though how many times have you seen some idiot 'profit ratio' depending on some dodgy profit figure?)

What E. Cary Brown demonstrated was that the economic rent earned by a company can be calculated very simply. Note that this discussion is conducted in terms of calculating the Brown Tax base, which is equivalent to calculating the value of the economic rent of a company.

How to calculate the Economic Rent of a company

Variables required

The aim of this exercise is to define a set of variables for which you can obtain values from the Company Annual Financial Statement. Then plug these values into a simple formula. And lo! You have obtained the value of economic rents.

The Brown Tax Formula

The standard Brown Tax formula is - Economic Rents equals Revenue R, less, Expenses E less the interest payments i, and less the Capital Expenditure C. (For a mathematical proof turn to chapter 14).

$$\sigma = R - (E - i) - C$$ Where

σ is economic rent
R is total revenue
E is total current expenses
i is interest payments
C is total capital expenditure

Note the interest paid i is deducted from the Expenses E. In other words, unlike the current corporation tax, interest expenses are **not** deductible!

The other big difference is that capital expenditure **is 100% deductible**. In other words there is 100% depreciation on all capital.

Thus if a Brown Tax was introduced to replace the current corporation tax, there would be big differences. But remember we are not talking about taxes, but economic rents. To repeat, the Brown Tax base is the same as the value of the company economic rent.

That's how you calculate economic rent.

There are minor issues with the definitions of the variables. These issues are explained below.

Step 1. The definition of revenue.

1.Total sales and service income. I prefer total or gross sales to net sales, as all returns etc. should appear under expenses. Net sales is gross sales less the deduction of returns, allowances for damaged or missing good or any discounts allowed. The difference in practice is minor.
2. Add any sales of fixed capital assets.
3. Any cash revenue from any source.
4. This revenue figure must include all interest receipts.

Step 2. Deduct all the normal current deductions as conducted under the current Corporation Tax.
Except interest payments. Interest payments are NOT deducted!

Step 3. Deduct 100% of all capital expenditure for that year. That is, 100% depreciation or capital expensing. Wow! Isn't that good news? What is industry moaning about? I'll show you later how to calculate this figure of capital expenditure from the published measures of asset values and depreciation.

The above is the standard Brown Tax base, and the measure of the value of economic rents.

A major issue is the treatment of **share issues** by the firm, **borrowings** and **repayment of borrowings**. The answer is simple. All capital increases by the firm are not considered part of the firm's income, and under a Brown Tax are not taxed. Therefore if a firm borrows, the cash inflow is not considered a part of its economic rent. Similarly a repayment of borrowings is ignored. Similarly the cash received by the firm from a share issue is not considered part of the firm's economic rents, and any share repurchases are ignored for the purpose of calculating economic rents.

In later chapters (Chapters 13 and 14) I will go over the economic theory and mathematical proof the Brown Tax/economic rent base. If you get glazed eyes from the use of mathematics and economic theory jump over these two chapters. You can also get the advice of your friendly local economist. Warning – you will find it hard getting an expert in this subject, as tax theory (which that section is) is an arcane subject that few follow.

Chapter 3

Finding the Annual Reports,
and about the 10-K

The next two chapters cover two aspects of the same subject. This chapter is on the vexed topic of actually finding the company financial reports/statements. The following Chapter 4 covers extracting the figures for total income, capital sales, total current deductions, interest payments, total assets in years one and two, and depreciation.

No, Virginia, companies just don't hand you the Financial Statements on a plate. "Oh, they are just in the Annual Reports!" Finding a Financial Statement is, for most companies, made hard and difficult. Only a few small companies with good profits make their financial statements easy to find. If you employ someone to find the company financial statements, give them a piece of leather to put between their teeth and double their salaries. If you find someone who does the job of finding financial statements rapidly and well, they are worth their weight in gold!

Financial Reports/Statements are usually located towards the end of the Company Annual Report. You need to find the Annual Report of that company for the latest year published.

In many countries, such as the US, Quarterly Reports are published. As a source of financial information these reports suffer for three reasons:
1. They are not audited, thus they are likely to be inaccurate (a lot more than the audited reports).
2. In many cases the figures reported are erratic and unstable. This could be because of the above-mentioned cause of inaccuracy of the report, or seasonal effects.

Private aggregators

I am aware of the existence of private aggregators and providers of company information, who can more easily provide the Annual Report information required. These sources are used by large funds and investors. If you have access to this information, lucky you. However these aggregator services are expensive. Unless you are very wealthy or run a large investment fund, it is unlikely that you can afford these aggregator services, and I am writing this book to explain how even a small investor can improve their investment performance without great expense.

ACCESSING FINANCIAL REPORTS

So you don't have access to the proprietary data sets (I won't name them, but most are very good), and you need to go directly to the source, the Company Annual Reports.

Nowadays, these Annual Reports are available on the internet, on the company web sites. But often the Annual Reports can be found on the company web site only with a great deal of difficulty, as they are well hidden. I have found that as a general rule, if the company has problems, - financial, management, cultural, - a number of obstructions are placed in front of you to prevent you accessing any useful financial results.

SEC Reports – the EDGAR site and the 10-K

However in the US, listed companies are required to file and publish a very useful annual financial reporting form with the Securities Exchange Commission (SEC), the 10-K. This information can be found on the SEC web site, called EDGAR, though the same information and form is sometimes also published on the company web site. The 10-K contains the Annual Financial Report, usually in a standard format together with a massive amount of detailed operational information. Even so, some firms, deliberately I think, try to make it difficult to access financial information even from this source. Be warned. In over 90% of these cases I have found, where you have access problems, the company is what I call 'dodgy'. Your eventual Economic Rents figures, obtained after much persistence, will confirm this. So it is dangerous to give up!

So, how does one find the 10-K? Type in to your search engine SEC EDGAR. The page you find is one of several SEC web sites that allow you to search for a particular company.

Type in the company name (not the stock exchange code) into the search box near the top of the page, and press 'enter'. The search engine comes up with a list of similar sounding companies. (There are many, many, companies in the investment galaxy, and while having identical names is forbidden, similar sounding names are allowed.) Choose the company you think it is and double click.

You get another list. Dozens, even hundreds of cryptic titles, 4-Q, 4-K, 8-K, many others. You would think American companies have nothing better to do except file reports with the SEC! They are filed in date order, the most recent first. Anyway, look for 10-K.

If you can't find 10-K, and you often can't, there is another search box at the top. Type in 10-K and enter.

You now get a reduced list, most of which are 10-K's. Select the one at the top, which is the most recent, and double click that.

You then get the standard SEC title page with the name of the company. Scroll down to the index page, which is the next page or two. You will immediately see that the SEC report is massive. Most of that stuff is of limited use to you, unless you are 1. An expert in company law. 2. You know what you are looking for. 3. You have invested in the company and suspect the company directors of malfeasance, or you think something strange is going on. The "risks" pages are always interesting, and are good for a laugh if nothing else. No, to be serious, the company is covering itself for EVERYTHING, and can claim "YOU HAVE BEEN INFORMED AND WARNED"

An alternative search method to going directly to the SEC web site is to Google the company name and 10-K. This often takes you directly there.

Go down the SEC report index, and down near the end you get "Section 8,……Page…..   Financial Statement"

Scroll down to that page. Down, down, past all the list of options the directors have awarded themselves, and the antics they get up to. (Insider trading is just the start of it!)

The Financial Statement is quite brief, and is in turn divided in three sections.

1. Revenue (The Income Statement).
2. The Balance Sheet.
3. The Cash Flow Statement.

The financial statements are usually highlighted in blue in the 10-K form, but are not otherwise very long. You get a few figures from each of the Cash Flow Statement, Revenue Statement and the Balance Sheet, as will be shown in the next chapter.

Company Annual Reports

The alternative method (especially if the company is not quoted in the US) is to access Annual Reports from the company web site. (There are special SEC report forms for foreign companies quoted in the US, the 20-K and the 20-F. It is still more worthwhile to look at these than the foreign company Annual Reports, which can be quite peculiar).

Publicly quoted companies must publish their own Annual Reports each year, which they usually publish on their company web site. This is very much a public relations exercise, and sometimes the actual financial statements are well hidden.

Indeed some offending companies fail to publish important figures in their financial statements. They give summaries which hide expenses in "Total Expenses" and so on. If this happens look in the SEC report, which requires obligatory figures; or from my wide experience, I suggest giving these companies a wide berth. There is plenty more fish in the sea. Do not invest in firms with incomplete financials.

Exercise in finding a Company Financial Report/Statement

As already discussed, finding a company financial report/statement is not easy. Actually it can be a real pain. You need a lot of experience to track them down quickly.

I suggest that from here on, as an exercise, that you open a company web site, and refer to it as I go through the method. Any company. General Electric for example.

Look up General Electric on Google and find their home web page. Look on the top right hand corner of the 'ribbon' at the top and for a small address "Investor services". (As I said, this not going to be easy). The address Investor services is also full of public relations stuff, but if you hunt around you can find a reference to Annual Reports. (No you don't want Quarterly Reports – remember what I said – they are un-audited and full of guff). Find the latest year's Annual Report and open it.

So you have found the latest company Annual Report web site. You are still not there by a country mile. The Annual Report will be really gee wiz, and try to impress you, or try to sell you stuff. But tucked away in a tiny corner is the address of the location of the company Financial Statement. It is up to you to find it. Don't worry, after a time you will become quite expert at squirreling it out. But for a beginner it can be frustrating. But it must be there. It is a legal requirement nowadays for all companies to place the Financial Statement on its web site. (But not make it easy to access. Some very well known companies seem to go out of their way to make it all but impossible to view their financial results. As I have said frequently, don't invest in such companies).

So it is worth repeating the process.

So Step 1. Look at the company home page. Look for a 'ribbon' giving the list of additional pages of the web site. This ribbon is usually at the top of the opening page, but various recalcitrant companies try to hide it at the bottom, and you have to scroll down to find it.

Remember what I said. The more difficult a company makes it to find their Financial Statement, the more likely they are to be in trouble. The combination of dishonesty and stupidity cannot be gainsaid. But nevertheless it is worth persisting to confirm this.

Step 2. In this ribbon you usually see a heading 'Investor information', 'investor', or such like, or this heading can be hidden under a heading 'Company Information'.

Step 3. Open this investor page. You are not there yet. You now get a whole list of reports and other publications. Most of these are useless for our purpose. Look for 'Annual Reports', or better still 'Annual Report year such and such' – then choose the Annual Report with the latest year.

Some of these other reports are Quarterly Reports. Ignore those. But if you get Report 10-K (latest year) that is pure gold. Open that. It contains a massive amount of detailed information about what the Directors are up to, but scroll down towards (see the section above) the end when you get to two pages – Revenue, and Balance Sheet. That's all you need,

Step 4. Many poor punters just get a web page of the Annual Report, or an Adobe pdf, or some complicated site that makes it very difficult to navigate – a warning sign already discussed. OK, ignore the bright pictures and try to find the index. This should give the page in the Annual Report at which the Financial Statement is situated. Invariably it is near the end of the Annual Report. Scroll down to this page.

But as I said, if the company is American, the best bet is to go directly to the SEC 10-K. The financial report is not hidden, and it is in a standard format.

How to obtain each set of accounting information is described in detail in the forthcoming chapter.

Chapter 4

The process of extracting the data from published Company Accounts

Got over the non-deductibility of interest payments? The 100% deduction of capital expenditure? Your head spinning? You are about to get in touch with your Congressman? Well don't worry. There is less chance of the Brown Tax being enacted, in the USA at least, than the moon being made of cheese. But you can gain from discovering which companies are earning high economic rents, even if this information is not reflected in their Profits Statement or Balance Sheet.

The method to calculate the Brown Tax Base is identical to calculating the economic rent! The reason is that the Brown Tax Base **is** the economic rent.

So lets run through the process of calculating the economic rent of a company, then describe how to automate this process so that you could in principle do it easily for the 5,000 or so quoted companies.

Now remember, we need five sets of data:

1. Total income.
2. Capital sales.
3. Total 'normal' or current deductions.
4. Interest payments.
5. Capital expenditure

The formula

The formula stated above is again as follows

$$\sigma = R - (E - i) - C$$

where

σ is economic rent
R is total revenue
E is total current expenses
i is interest payments
C is total capital expenditure

It is very rare to find Capital Sales figures, but if you do, just add them to Total Revenue.

The process of data extraction

This data is extracted from the latest published Financial Statements of public companies. These Financial Reports almost invariably follow a standard form required by the international accounting bodies. This means that they fall into three parts, an Income and Profits Statement, a Balance sheet, and a Cash Flow Statement. The contents of these parts have basic standard requirement, though the details vary quite considerably between company and company and country and country.

Nowadays the vast majority of these companies publish these Annual Reports on their Web Sites. Alternatively, as described in the previous chapter, if the company is American, use the SEC 10-K publication of the company's financial statement.

Revenue

We go straight to the Cash Flow Statement. Why? Because the Revenue figure in the Income Statement can be doctored to some degree by the clever accountants. Not so much as the Profit, but it can be "adjusted". Furthermore, many companies publish a "Net Revenue" figure only. You need a figure for all the cash flowing into the company. Remember you are essentially looking at cash flows.

If you can't find the Cash Flow Statement, use the Total Income figure in the Income Statement.

Often you can only find the Net Income figure. Net income is the Total Income adjusted for returns and stock losses. The difference between Net Income and Total Income is usually minor; but nevertheless, for the purpose of this book, I do no like this adjustment.

So the preferences for a Total Revenue figure in order are:
1. Total income from the Cash Flow Statement.
2. Total income from the Income Statement.
3. Net Income from the income statement.

It amazes me that three different figures can be given for the same thing, but there you are, that's accounting.

There you are. Simple. With these figures you can calculate an unambiguous value of the Economic Rents.

Expenses. Total current expenses are found in the Income Statement, about half way down. Total expenses are deducted form the Total Sales in order to calculate Profits. Make sure you select the Current Expenses figure, and not capital adjustments such as depreciation.

Interest expense. This is normally in the Income Statement (but not always) among the expenses deducted form revenue to estimate profits. If it cannot be found (some company accounts for perverse reasons grossly summarize expenses) look in the Financial Section of the Cash flow Statement, or if it is not there, you may find it in the Notes. US banks have got into habit of hiding both interest income and interest expenses (and a lot else). If that happens obtain the figure for Total Current and Long Term Borrowing in the Liabilities section of the Balance Sheet, and multiply this by some arbitrary interest rate to get a rough estimate.

Capital Expenditure. Most companies publish their Capital Expenditure figure in the "Cash Flow from Investing Activity" statement in the Cash Flow section of the accounts at the end of end of the Consolidated Financial Statement. . Such a figure is next to a term such as "Purchase of Property and Equipment" or just "Capital Expenditure".

Simple. However some firms are recalcitrant and do not publish these figures. These are mainly banks and financial institutions such as insurance companies, as usual. What does one do?

Conceptually in economics capital expenditure is the value of assets in year 2 less the value of assets in year 1 plus depreciation in year 2. Adding back depreciation takes account of the decline in accounting value of the asset in the intervening year.

Depreciation can be usually found in the "Cash Flow from Operating Activities" section.

However nothing is simple in accounting. Accountants have had a long-standing practice of re-valuing assets, up and down, but mainly up. They argue that this gives "the true picture of the position of the company". The reality is that revaluing assets upwards bolsters the accounting profit. Only rarely do they revalue assets downwards, and even more rarely, I have found, do they then revalue profits down.

What does this mean for the value of economic rents? Valuing asset values upwards increases the value of the calculated capital expenditure, but reduces the value of the calculated economic rent. (Capital expenditure is deducted from revenue). My opinion is that firms who habitually revalue assets to bolster their profits should in fairness show lower economic rents, so that these shares should comprise little or no part or your portfolio.

Yes, you may find in the Notes a figure for the revaluation amount to readjust asset values. This will take you a great deal of time and effort. It is generally not worth looking for it.

What if asset prices in year 2 are less than asset prices in year 1? This occasionally happens, especially if the company is doing badly. Unfortunately if asset prices in year 1 are deducted from asset prices in year 2, the result is often negative even if you add depreciation. BUT this has the effect of *increasing* measured economic rents. Obviously this is wrong, because a company that is devaluing its assets is normally doing badly, and its economic rents are likely to be low or negative.

Therefore in this very occasional case where the capital expenditure figure is not published *and* the calculated capital expenditure figure is negative, I recommend in the spreadsheet this negative figure is set to zero. This can be done automatically in Excel using a 'macro' "If this figure is negative then set to zero". If you can't do this yourself get someone to do it for you.

Capital sales is added to Revenue. Or it can be deducted from Capital Expenditure. It is published in the Cash flow Statement, but normally it is a very low figure. Take care to just use the figure for "Sales of Property and Equipment". Sales of financial investments are not counted in the calculations for the economic rent.

The following chapter is a practical calculation.

Chapter 5

A practical application

So how do you calculate the economic rents of an actual company? The following is an exercise in doing this. We shall use the accounts of a well-known company to do this – Apple.

APPLE

Lets look at Apple's current Annual Financial Report. For a US company I get this information from The Securities and Exchange Commission (SEC) published 10-K report. Highly convenient. The 10-K is the SEC standard form Annual Report.

For companies based in other countries you will have to go direct to their published Annual Reports, hopefully published on the internet.

So go to the SEC web site. In the search engine box type in "Apple 10-K". This will bring up a list of reports. Pick the latest 10-K.

You will find this report is massive. Check the title to see if you have got the right company and then scroll down, down, down, until you get nearly to the end. You get to the short section on published financial reports.

There will be three financial reports:

1. The Income and Profit and Loss Report
2. The Balance Sheet
3. The Cash Flow Statement.

DATA EXTRACTION

The following is an example of the type of data extracted from company accounts and used to calculate economic rents. In this case Apple.

Data extraction follows the list described in the previous chapter, and is for a single year (the latest) except for the calculation of Capital Expenditure when the latest year's depreciation figures are also extracted from the company accounts.

This particular table also has a column noting the source of this data in the Company Accounts. In practice, when you get more experienced you need not include this column in every table.

APPLE

Accounting Item	Source	2013	2012
		$ million	$ million
Total revenue (including interest received)	10-K Cash Flow Statement Consolidated Statement of Operations	170,910	
Current Expenses	10-K Consolidated Statement of Operations	106,606	
Interest expense	10 –K Note 3*	136	
Capital Expenditure	Cash Flow from Operating Activities	8165	

*For many company Annual Reports, Interest Expense can be found in the Income Statement, or failing that, the Cash Flow Statement. Apple placed this information in the Notes.

The calculation is as follows:

Remember the formula is:

$$\sigma = R - (E - i) - C$$

Where
σ is economic rent
R is total revenue
E is total current expenses
i is interest payments
C is total capital expenditure

The formula for Economic Rent is

$$\sigma = R - (E - i) - C$$

So
Economic Rents = Total Revenue – (Expenses – interest paid) – Capital Expenditure

Economic Rents = 170,910 – (106,606 – 136) – 8165

$$= 170,910 - 106,470 - 8165$$

$$= 56,275$$

This figure may be interesting, but it is meaningless, unless it can be compared to something.

Now economic rent is a measure of that part of total income that is rent.

Thus the métier is Total Revenue. Divide by Total Revenue to get a percentage figure. This percentage figure can be used to compare the level of rents of all enterprises.

Percentage economic rent = 56,275/170,910

$$= 33\%$$

That is Apple is making an economic rent on its income of 33%. Once you have calculated a large number of these economic rents, you will find that this level of economic rents is reasonable, though not exceptional. From the economic rent point of view, Apple is a good investment.

As will be seen this calculation can be automated using a spreadsheet. The spreadsheet has an additional advantage that it assists setting up an optimal portfolio, which also will be described.

Chapter 6

Using Spreadsheets

The above methodology can of course be extended to the use of a spreadsheet. I still recommend using the form described for Apple to extract the necessary data from company financial statements, but the spreadsheet can be used to make the necessary calculations. The spreadsheet can also be used to sort the final results, and as will be described, re-sort them in terms of the share price for inclusion in an optimal portfolio.

If you have never used a spreadsheet, nor do not understand how to properly construct one, it is not the purpose of this book to teach you. You must either learn (it is not hard), or the second best, get someone to do it for you. I recommend learning to do it yourself – being dependent on others for what is basically a simple and interesting task is foolish. Also if they make mistakes, you have no way of picking up on it.

So what is the design of this spreadsheet? It will be something like the form below.

SPREADSHEET COLUMN HEADINGS

Company name	Total Revenue	Total Current Expenditure	Interest Paid	Total current expenditure less interest paid	Capital Expenditure	Estimated Economic Rents	Economic rents as a percentage of total revenue

Remember again the formula is:

$$\sigma = R - (E - i) - C$$

where

σ is economic rent
R is total revenue
E is total current expenses
i is interest payments
C is total capital expenditure

A spreadsheet of selected real 2013 company financial results has been calculated and the results are shown in the next chapter.

Chapter 7

The Spreadsheet Results

The beauty and benefit of this spreadsheet is that you can get dozens of company results on one page. You can compare them against each other, sort the results into order of the increasing ratio of economic rents, and even manipulate the results by dividing them say by their current price/earnings ratios and re-sorting them.

This does away with the current investment selection method of going through tedious, and largely useless investment reports on each company. By the time you have read a dozen of these reports, you don't know how to make head or tail of them. Additionally there is no way to compare the companies, as each report will have at least half a dozen investment criteria, all different.

On the next page is an example of an Economic Rents spreadsheet. Yes, they are genuine company results. But a word of warning. By the time you read this book all these figures will be out of date, as they largely relate to the first half of the year 2013. Do not use these figures for your investment decisions. They are published for instructional purposes only. You must produce your own spreadsheet based on the latest Annual Reports, and of course, keep it up to date.

I suggest that you initially use as a guide for a list of quoted companies a publication such as the Fortune 500 list, and obtain from elsewhere your own financial information for each company. (The Fortune 500 list unfortunately has limited financial information).

I further suggest that you go away to a cabin in the woods and create a giant spreadsheet of the Fortune 500 companies. It will be a useful exercise, for there are more than enough companies with high economic rents in the Fortune 500 companies to construct a useful portfolio.

You will however have to set up your own spreadsheet. Unfortunately I can't stick an electronic gizmo into this book to do it for you. But I intend to set up a web site, with a spreadsheet of the Top 500 companies plus a number of others, which you can copy. Just do a Google search *economicrents.com* and it should pop up. The access to this web site will be free, but I cannot guarantee a frequent update. This spreadsheet should be of purely economic interest, and there will be no guidance provided on whether to buy or sell individual shares, as this decision will also depend on the individual share price and the risk per share, as well as your individual circumstance – and not only on the economic rent ratio.

Get the working of your spreadsheet checked by someone who knows these things. You don't want to make the wrong investment decisions because you set up the formulae wrong. However if you use the figures in the following spreadsheet as a test, it will be a demonstration that your spreadsheet works.

SPREADSHEET SHOWING ECONOMIC RENTS

Company name	Total Revenue	Total Current Expenditure	Interest Paid	Total Current Expenditure less Interest Paid	Capital Expenditure	Estimated Economic Rents	Economic Rents as a percentage of Total Revenue
Apple	170910	106606	136	106470	8165	56275	33
American Airlines	26743	25344	256	25088	2966	-1311	-5
Bank of America	95181	86051	10934	75117	2146	17918	19
BHP Billiton	65968	50873	1522	49351	21573	-4956	-8
BP	396217	365996	1068	364928	24250	7039	2
Boeing	86623	73268	386	72882	2047	11694	13
Chevron	228848	192943	250	192693	37985	-1830	-1
Citigroup	92543	48355	16177	32178	3490	56875	61
Delta Airlines	36670	34495	812	33683	2568	419	1
Exxon Mobil	438255	380544	9	380535	33669	24051	5
Ford	146917	141478	2860	138618	7360	939	1
General Electric	146045	129894	657	129237	7595	9213	6
General Motors	155427	150296	334	149962	7565	-2100	-1
Glencore	232694	227145	1781	225364	9451	-2121	-1
Goldman Sachs	34206	22469	6668	15801	706	17699	52
Hewlett Packard	112298	105617	621	104996	2546	4756	4
IBM	99751	51246	402	50844	3251	45656	46
Lockheed	45358	41171	350	40821	836	3701	8
McDonalds	28106	19341	522	18819	3566	5721	20
Microsoft	73723	51960	3100	48860	2305	22558	31
Rio Tinto	51171	36104	507	35597	13001	2573	5
Union Pacific	27988	15235	561	14674	4108	9206	33
Walmart	469162	441361	2251	439110	12366	17686	4

WARNING. These figures are out of date by the time you get them. DO NOT use these figures to make investment decisions.

Many will be shocked by these results. Their favorite shares, recommended by their stockbrokers, get the thumbs down, or at the very best, are a mediocre investment.

Well don't complain to me! As I said, these results are out of date. Re-estimate them yourself, using the latest Annual Report results.

However, one thing about these published numbers is that they are calculated correctly. If you plug these numbers into your own spreadsheet, you should get identical answers. This demonstrates that your spreadsheet works! Then you can modify these numbers with the latest figures.

The positive numbers in the right hand column denote that the firm is making an economic rent. Thus for Apple, the firm is making an economic rent of 33 cents for every dollar of sales. This is its _real_ profit.

The negative numbers denote that the firm is making a negative economic rent. Compare American Airlines, rent ratio - 5%, with Delta Airlines, which manages to achieve + 1%. Another transport company, Union Pacific, makes healthy rents, rent ratio 33%, no doubt because it keeps its wheels on the ground!

As I have said, this spreadsheet is deliberately out of date to prevent you using these results for investing. I am aware that since these figures were calculated, American Airlines has merged with United. There is some evidence since of greater margins and better management, but if you a thinking of investing in this merged airline, I advise you take its latest financial results and run them on this spreadsheet.

Banks normally have very high rents, because of the nature of their business. They actually print money, and currently they are offered money by the government bearing little or no interest. However they are also highly risky as the have very high leverage. As a consequence I do not recommend that you invest a high proportion of your portfolio in banks. Banks are the exception to the rule that high rents equal a safe investment.

In a later chapter, there will be a discussion about risk, and how to structure your portfolio. However this process is complicated and time consuming. If you have a relatively small portfolio (under $1 million) I suggest that if you are going to weight your portfolio in proportion to the economic rent ratios, you arbitrarily deduct 40 from the economic rent ratios of banks. This is arbitrary. If you want to be really safe deduct 50 or more. The basic message is, avoid investing in banks as a significant proportion of your portfolio.

The process of adjusting the proportions of shares in your portfolio is discussed in Chapter 9.

Some people may become impatient with the discussion of risk and portfolios in the forthcoming chapters. Ignoring this advice is your choice, but let me say, choosing the right shares to invest in is only part of the process. You also need to optimize your choices. You gain more advantage from doing this, and this advantage accumulates over the years.

Chapter 8

Constructing the Optimal Portfolio

This chapter describes how to construct a non-risk weighted portfolio. For most investors, this is probably the simplest outcome for a weighted portfolio, if you want to weight your portfolio at all. My advice is that it is worth weighting your portfolio as described, if your portfolio value exceeds $100,000. (That low). The steady gains from doing this accumulate considerably over time.

So you have done your research (yeech!), constructed a massive spreadsheet, and from this you have selected a list of suitable shares you are interested in investing in. Well done!

Yes, you can go out in a fit of enthusiasm and buy a selection of these chosen shares. There is no harm in doing that, though check the p/e ratios. But lets assume that you have a heap of cash and want to construct an 'optimal portfolio'. Just to get the last ounce of investment gain out of the system. How do you do that?

Basically you need to buy shares in proportion to their measures of the value of the ratio of economic rents, and in inverse proportion to their relative price. The higher the economic rents ratio, the more shares you buy, and higher the relative price the fewer shares you buy. (I won't go into such issues as the variability of the share prices, beta, and so on. This chapter's method is for a 'do it yourself' portfolio, and the suggested method is in my opinion perfectly adequate for most investment portfolios under $1 million.)

What is the best measure of relative price? Obviously there is a vast range of share prices, depending on the units of their shares.

There are many measures that are independent of the unit of the shares such as the price earnings ratio (p/e), or the dividend yield, or earnings to cash ratio, and so on. I have found by far the best measure of price is the p/e ratio, and the foregoing discussion will be conducted in terms of the p/e ratio. But don't let this stop you using another measure according to your needs. Just substitute this measure into the term p/e ratio in the foregoing discussion. The methodology will work just the same.

So. More work. (sigh!). Another spreadsheet. (groan!).

This spreadsheet will be much smaller and simpler than the previous one. But three major advantages will stem from its use.

1. The distribution of shares in your portfolio will have a distribution biased towards shares that are the most likely to be safe.
2. It incorporates a system of regularly revising and renewing the share portfolio.
3. And lastly, described in a later chapter, it incorporates a 'trip wire', which tells you when to liquidate the share portfolio into cash at the height of a share boom, before it crashes. These share crashes are regular occurrences, yet people rely on nothing more than instinct for choosing the time when to bail out. As a consequence most lose out!

Right. Lets set up this spreadsheet. It consists of eight columns. 1. Company name. 2. The latest economic rents measure of the company. 3. The latest p/e ratio of company (obtained from an alternative source such as a newspaper). 4. The ratio of the economic rents of the company by the p/e ratio of the company. 5. Percentage weight of each share. 6. Actual value of these shares. 7. Desired weighted value of each share. 8. Difference. Sell −. Buy +.

This spreadsheet is shown in the diagram below.

Company name	Economic rents ratio of company	Latest p/e ratio of company	Economic rents ratio of the company/pe ratio of the company	Percentage desired weight of the holding of each share %	Actual value of all the shares held of this company $	Desired weighted value of all the shares held of this company $	Difference. Sell −. Buy +.

The explanation of these column names is as follows:

Column	Explanation
Company name	Name of the company shares
Economic rents ratio of company	The calculated economic rents ratio that company*
P/e ratio of company	Current p/e ratio of that company obtained from a daily media source
Economic rents ratio of company/pe ratio of company	The economic rents ratio divided by the p/e ratio
Percentage desired weight of the holding of each share	This percentage desired weight ratio is obtained by dividing the above obtained ratio by the sum of all the ratios in the portfolio, and converting it into a percentage figure
Actual value of each of all the shares held of this company	Number of that company's shares in the portfolio x current market price
Desired weighted value of all the shares held of this company	The desired weighted value of each share is obtained by multiplying the percentage weight of each share by the current portfolio value of all the shares in the portfolio (sum of actual value of each of these shares in the portfolio)
Difference. Sell −. Buy +.	This is the value of the shares of that company which should be sold or bought to restore the portfolio to an 'optimum' distribution. It is

found by subtracting the actual value of each of these shares from the desired weighted value of each of these shares.

* To save a bit of effort, a link for the economic rents ratio can be connected to the previous spreadsheet. So when that figure changes, so does the one in this spreadsheet change.

So there you are. This spreadsheet may look complicated, but if you can't set it up yourself, ask a person moderately competent in spreadsheets to construct it.

When you initially purchase your portfolio of shares, I recommend that you use this spreadsheet to allocate the proportions of each share you will purchase for the portfolio. As you see, by dividing by the p/e ratio, there is a bias towards the less expensive shares. There is a very good reason for this. Less expensive shares, with lower p/e ratios, are more likely to rise in price! So are shares with a higher economic rents ratio. Thus your portfolio is biased towards shares of companies with higher economic rents ratios and lower p/e ratios.

But as I said constructing and maintaining this spreadsheet is well worth the effort. You will be immediately on top of all your share investments. Furthermore you will automatically buy and sell shares when necessary.

However, as noted in the previous chapter, if you do not use the method described in the following chapter for risk weighting the portfolio, at least adjust down the economic rents ratio of banks by 40, as they have a higher level of risk because of their high leverage. This will weight down the proportion of banks in the portfolio. The other high-risk companies are adjusted down pro-rata. A bad fright recently during the financial crisis impelled me to do this. Over recent years it has become apparent to me that banks have become a lot more risky, and I feel that investment in the banking sector at least should be proportionately reduced. It is recommended that you do some risk adjustment downwards for bank holdings.

Now, how often should your portfolio be revised?

This should be done regularly, at least every six months for a small portfolio, and more frequently for a large portfolio.

However the Economic Rents Ratio for each company should be recalculated as soon as its Annual Report is published. This is important as it happens quite often that a change in the economic rents ratio measure has occurred. Sometimes for the worst. What happens is that after a good year, management often gets a rush of blood to the head, and starts splashing out on assets, or hiring staff like mad. If this happens it is best to reduce your holding of these shares immediately before the rest of the world realizes. So re-weight the holding using the method described above, and reduce your holding. If you are in a hurry, just reduce the share by the ratio of the old and new economic rents ratio measure, and do a general re-weighting later.

The aim of regularly reweighting the portfolio is to automatically readjust the portfolio for both changes in price and changes in economic rents. In most cases minor changes can maintain an optimal mix of the existing shares in the portfolio.

I also recommend a system of constant renewal of the share portfolio. I have found this is a very necessary exercise. It is too easy to rest on one's laurels. Out with the old and in with the new!

I remove the shares with the lowest economic rents ratios, and replace them with shares with better ratios. Up to three shares every six months in a thirty share portfolio.

I usually do this on a regular, not continuous, basis as you have to adjust the proportions of all the shares in the portfolio at the same time. There is a big question of stockbrokers' commissions. For portfolios up to a million dollars once every six months is enough.

If I find a 'good' investment with a high ratio, I usually don't buy immediately, but I add it to a list to be used on the regular revision date. But this is up to you.

Chapter 9

Risk
– or adjusting the Portfolio for 'Beta'

If you don't want to adjust you portfolio further for risk, jump this chapter. My advice is that unless you have a portfolio worth well over $1 million it is not worth the effort. The gains from adjusting for risk are too small to make it worthwhile.

The definition below of 'Beta' is taken is taken from Investopedia, a web site source of investment terms.

Beta, also known as the 'beta coefficient', is a measure of volatility, or systemic risk, of a security or portfolio in comparison to the market as a whole. Beta is calculated using regression analysis, and you can think of it as a tendency of an investment's return to respond to swings in the market. By definition, the market has a beta of 1.0. Individual security and portfolio values are measured according to how they deviate from the market.

A beta of 1.0 indicates that the investment will move in lock-step with the market. A beta of less than 1.0 indicates that that investment will be less volatile than the market, and, correspondingly, a beta of more than 1.0 indicates that the investment's price will be more volatile than the market. For example, if a fund portfolio's beta is 1.2, it is theoretically 20% more volatile than the market.

Conservative investors looking to preserve capital should focus on securities and fund portfolios with low betas, whereas those investors willing to take on more risk in search of higher returns should look for high beta investments.

Now the Beta for individual banks, and indeed the beta of the banking industry as a whole can be measured. The Bank of England has measured the beta for the Bank of America, Citibank and Goldman Sachs, for instance, and has found them to be currently around 2 for the first two banks, and 2.5 for Goldman Sachs. In other words by this measure banks are twice as risky as the general share market!

There are useful sources of betas for individual companies.

These are:

1. The ICAEW Library and Information Services data base. This service provides data on selected company betas in print form on a quarterly basis for a fee. They can be contacted on library@lcaew.com
2. The London Business School (University of London) Risk Measurement Service (LBS) maintains a database of beta values for 3000 UK companies. Go to the London Business School Website – Risk Management service (RMS). Again a fee based service.
3. The Financial Analysis Made Easy (FAME) data base form Bureau Van Dijk (BVD) includes beta values for most publicly listed companies. Again you have to pay, but it is a pretty complete coverage.

Finally if you employ a share charting service, and have access to a few years' daily data, but preferably weekly share data for the chosen company, the program probably has a nifty sub-program that will calculate the beta for you. It is probably cheaper doing this than using the above databases, but requires a bit more effort and is more time consuming. My personal preference is for people to do as much for themselves as possible – there is less risk of error involved.

Adjusting your share portfolio for betas.

As I said at the start, unless you have a $1 million plus portfolio, adjusting for risk, except for arbitrarily reducing the proportion of bank shares, is not usually worth the time and effort.

So – what do you have? You have a set of shares with calculated economic rent ratios. Also you have the betas or those shares.

What to do? Basically it is very simple. You are going to adjust the proportions of your shares in your portfolio in inverse relation to the size of the betas. The higher the beta, the greater the risk. The lower the beta the beta, the lower the risk. The neutral beta is equal to 1.

Step 1. Divide 1 by each of the betas of the individual companies.
Step 2. Convert each of these values into a percentage by adding all these values together, dividing each of these values by this total, and multiplying by 100.
Step 3. All these percentage figures give the risk-weighted proportion of these shares in your portfolio.

As shown in the previous chapter you can estimate the percentage share of each share in you portfolio to a price earnings ratio adjusted optimum. Basically you just divided the economics rent ratio by the p/e ratio, totaled it, and divided by this total to obtain a percentage weight.

You now have two sets of percentage figures for each share, the risk weighted percentage measure, and the p/e adjusted percentage measure.

Do you want to adjust this portfolio for beta risk weighting? If so, how do you combine them? Additive, or multiplicative?

Multiplicative. Each of these percentage values is a weight.

Step 1. You multiply both percentage weights for each share to get a product value.
Step 2. Add all the products together to obtain a total.
Step 3. You divide each product by this total.
Step 4. You multiply the result of this division for each share by 100. This gives the combined risk weighted and p/e weighted proportion for each share in the portfolio.

There you are. The risk weighted, p/e weighted optimal portfolio.

An academic diversion on the value of betas.

Being a poor economist, I raise these academic diversions. Only if you are running a multi-million dollar fund do you need to bother to read to the end of this chapter. This is all about adjusting the size of the betas, and the gain for most investors doing this will be negligible.

One problem in the use of betas is that there is an almost universal assumption that the relationship between risk and the size of the betas is *linear*. As a matter of fact, this relationship is *non-linear*. As the size of the beta increases the size of the risk increases at a more rapid pace. It even can be said that the size of the risk increases exponentially.

In other words there is no direct relationship between the variance in the share price and the risk of that share. Professors of Finance argue that the variance *is* the risk. Full stop. End of story. All you are interested in is the share price. A little thought will show that there is a lot more to risk involved in investing in a company's share than just the possible downward movement in the share price.

How do I explain this? It is a well-known feature of experimental economics (the discovery of this concept was the reason why Daniel Kahneman won a Nobel Prize in Economics in 2001) that humans tend to under-estimate risk. People over estimate their own capabilities, have a limited grasp of the implications of probability theory, and have a foreshortened time horizon. So in particular, if a particular share is risky, the market (made up of human traders) undervalues that risk. Thus if the variance of a share, and its derivation the beta, is used as a value of risk; since this value is created in the market it *underrates* the size of the risk of that share, especially at the end where beta is high. "Risk" could include sudden drops in earnings, unforeseen disasters (your oil rig explodes), international risks to the company activities, domestic government risk, collapse of the economy, etc.

Thus, in your portfolio, if the proportions are adjusted by the straight betas derived from price movements, (as, it often done in many portfolios and funds, the p/e ratios are adjusted down by the size of the beta), the portfolio is still excessively risky. **The market-based indicator of risk, the beta, still causes an excessively risky outcome.** The beta only *partially* measures the higher risks. There has to be a greater adjustment of the portfolio, than by just using the estimated values of the beta, to fully compensate for risk.

What can be done about it? One way is to re-size the betas in a non-linear manner. This is to look at share performance over the long term, say 30 years, for various currently high beta companies, and re-weight these values up-wards. But this process is very technical and is up there in the realms of academia.

A second method is to arbitrarily increase the betas using some arbitrary curve. I suggest using some form of a fractal probability distribution curve as the best measure, as it has fat tails and in my opinion reflects reality better. Ie Draw a straight line for the current beta values, and apply a fractal probability curve to it, and use those new beta values as a substitute for the equivalent straight-line betas.

As I said at the beginning of this chapter, if you have a relatively small portfolio, say under $1 million dollars in value, in my opinion you won't gain much by adjusting your entire portfolio for betas compared to the quick and easy method described above of reducing the weight of the banks by reducing the ratio by 40 and leaving the rest unadjusted.

And only if you have a multi-million dollar portfolio is it worth playing around with the value of the betas.

Chapter 10

Are Share Prices more stable for Companies with high Economic Rents?

This is the elephant in the room. Are share prices more stable for companies with a high level of economic rents? Are these shares safer than most company shares?

The answer is that generally share prices for these companies are more stable than the market. Yes, they do go up and down with the movements of the share market, especially as some of these companies are large and make a sizable component of the share index. But the price of these shares will not drop through the floor as their profits evaporate in difficult times, like those of General Motors. By conducting this process of estimating economic rents, you are conducting a winnowing effect, and confining your share investments to the safest sector of the market.

I could at this point give a demonstration by listing the performance, or more precisely the betas (a measure of variability), of a number of high economic rent ratio companies and compare them to the performance of the market in general. I have not done this because such a demonstration would be effectively a recommendation to buy using outdated information. I am very careful not to make individual share purchase advice in this book as in many parts of the world such advice on my part would be illegal, as I am not a licensed share adviser. **It is up to you, the individual investor, to check the recent share price performance of these companies and relate that performance to the market as a whole.**

What should you do? Nothing onerous. I suggest that you download from the internet a chart of the company's share price over the last five years (there are numerous free sites which allow you to do this), and download a chart of a suitable index, such as Dow Jones or S&P, and compare.

Now "eye balling" is more than adequate. The human brain is built to obtain a lot more information from a picture than any number of mathematical measures. You will see in front of you the relative volatility, price rises and falls or stability when the rest of the market falls, upward trends in a downward market, all those thing which will show whether this share is a good investment.

Misuse of various technical and mathematical measures, such betas, without a good understanding of the basis on what they are measured, such as most importantly the frequency of the data set (it must not be daily for long term investment purposes), causes a lot of grief and bad decision making. Believe me, comparing charts is far better. However, as related in a previous chapter, a list of betas for many companies are available from several sources. If for a variety of reasons (including laziness) you don't wish to use my suggested chart method, the use of a list of betas is better than nothing.

Why not just use charts to find good investments? Because the economic rents method give a reason <u>why</u> certain charts are more stable. The good share performance of a particular share is not just based on spin and fashion.

I suppose this is a good place for a **Disclaimer**. If the method I have described in this book is applied conscientiously and the methodology is completely followed without error; over the medium term with an adequate portfolio of shares, losses are likely to be minimized and profits are likely to be made. The author does not guarantee that you will not make losses in all circumstances, or will make profits at a particular period. Markets are not completely rational over short periods of time, and 'acts of god' and extreme events beyond the control of any person can occur. You are solely responsible for all the investment decisions you make. This book only describe a general method to make good investments, and provides no advice on individual shares beyond indicating a way to select good share investments and allocating the selected share into a proportion of your share portfolio.

Chapter 11

Avoiding Ruin,
or at least the harmful effects of a
General Share Crash

What! Avoid ruin! I thought this method you describe almost guarantees that you will avoid losing money. What is this talk about ruin?

Yes, dear reader, that is correct. But you will have noticed that on average every ten years the share market goes into a frenzy, rises to a peak (very nice), and then suddenly without warning crashes 30 or 40% (not so nice). All those shares you bought at or near the peak have lost money. How devastating!

A rational reader would say to me, well that is not your fault. After all, the aim of the book is to teach you to pick good shares, with the not inconsiderable hope that they will at least not fall in price as much as other shares. The periodic share crashes are beyond anyone's control.

True, that is one way of looking at it. However, dear reader, I DO want to see you retire to a prosperous old age, and if you have got this far, and have applied the methodology which I have described, I will feel guilty if I have left you with a situation where periodically all your hard work comes to (near) naught, and you have to wait several years for recovery. That is the usual fate of all share investors, even if they have invested well.

While this economic rent methodology described is an excellent way of avoiding the worst of the share crash, as these shares would tend not to fall so much, and indeed it is a great way of picking good shares at the bottom, wouldn't it be better to keep your top of the market gains, and prevent the subsequent losses?

But don't be dismayed. I shall finish this chapter with a description of an automatic signal, a trip wire, which will save your hard earned earnings before a market crash. Read carefully.

First of all, you have noticed that you have a method of automatically selling shares from your portfolio shares with a high relative p/e value, and re-basing your portfolio.

But what happens when all the shares in the portfolio have a high p/e value? No matter how hard you try, everything in your portfolio seems to be traded up to the sky? Then it is the time to get out. Cash up. Put the money into government bonds (if the return is 4% p.a. or more). Sit on it. Wait.

What level should you sell? I have a magic figure. If the average p/e of your portfolio is **20** or more, sell the lot. This will give a buffer for risk.

Why twenty?

When a p/e is 20, the earnings rate of return to capitalization is 5%. This is equal to the 'risk adjusted' rate of return of long-term government stocks. Even with a potential further rise in portfolio values it is not worth taking this risk. Remember you are playing with your retirement money.

Surely most shares in your portfolio at the top of the bubble will have a p/e greater than 20? Not just half, most.

Here, bear with me, as I go into a bit more economic speak, or you can jump ahead and just do what I say. The average p/e is matter of the distribution of p/e's in your portfolio, and the shape of that distribution. Remember you have been selling a high proportion of the shares with a relatively high p/e and buying shares with a low p/e.

Imagine a chart of the p/e's of the shares in your portfolio as a graph with the measure of the p/e's as the x axis, and the value of shares as the y axis. The graph will be in the form of a curve, with the highest point to the left, and descending to the right. The shares with the lowest p/e's will have the most invested in them. Why? Because you have been regularly re-basing your portfolio, so that most of the money in the portfolio is in shares with a low p/e.

Thus the average p/e will not be in the middle of the curve, the average p/e of all the shares, but moved to the left, the weighted value of the p/e's.

What do you mean by "average"? I mean the "weighted average", weighted by the total value of each share in your portfolio. How do you weight the shares?

1. Multiply the value of each share by the p/e of that share.
2. Add all these products together.
3. Add up the actual values of all the shares in the portfolio to obtain a total.
4. Now this is important, divided the weighted total above by the second portfolio total to get a weighted average p/e.

It's not hard. You can actually set up the spreadsheet to do it for you each time.

So, when the weighted average p/e of your continuously revised economic rents portfolio, constructed in the method described above, reaches 20, SELL ALL.

The majority of the share in your portfolio will have a p/e of over 20, and will be over priced.

From long experience, the mean long term p/e of shares are something like 15. This is your warning bell. Soon, very soon, the share market will crash. DON'T get greedy and hang on!

Alternatively just total up all the p/e's in your portfolio and divide by the number of companies you have invested in in the portfolio. As described above you will get an upward bias in the average p/e, but that is an error on the safe side. Sell if the average p/e of the portfolio is above 20.

Chapter 12

Finding shares to invest in, Share Tips, Dividends, and assorted further advice

How does one find new shares to invest in?

You have started by using the massive spreadsheet method at the start. It is the sledgehammer approach, but after you have analyzed the Top 500 you have picked a number of shares to invest in. No, you don't want to go through that process again, unless you are that unusual person that loves doing that sort of thing. But you have gained two major assets:

1. Knowledge that a large number of the top 500 companies are investment junk, and are not worth investing in.
2. You have a spreadsheet that will work out the economic rents of any new company you will find.

However, if you want to keep going for another 10,000 quoted companies, don't let me stop you. This chapter is aimed at other readers who want to stay sane.

So you have done the Top 500. But there are loads of others. How do you hear about them?

Free tips? No! If you get a free tip from some public source as an internet site, newspaper article, or TV or radio program, you are either at the end of the line or somebody else wants to sell and wants the bunnies to support the market. Very very occasionally the tipsters pass out something good, but only to maintain their record "I recommended so-and-so which increased 40%!" All these tips are worth checking with this economic rents methodology, but don't hold your breath.

Investment magazines, and paid for investment advice services, whether internet or hard copy, especially specialist ones, are a better bet. It is worthwhile subscribing. On the subject of subscriptions I know many investors who are personally "cheap". They won't spend money on subscriptions, either paper or the internet. Now paid for investment tips are vastly more valuable than the free variety, for the simple reason that the writers of these have to perform to make a living. It is better to subscribe to a service for a limited period, and test the recommendations, than not subscribe at all. If at the end of 12 months, if the service does not come up to desired quality, give them a chop. As a rule of thumb, I have unsubscribed about half of the internet investment services I have signed up for. And about ten per cent of the hard copy magazines.

As for the 'cheap' investors who won't subscribe to investment services, they lose most of their money in the end. If you go near them, they complain, and blame anyone but himself or herself.

Other sources of investment ideas are serendipity. A news report mentions a company in a particular context. Write it down. A friend mentions a share. It is amazing how many good investment ideas pop up this way. But always check them out using the spreadsheet.

Finally your stockbroker. Well the dear old stockbroker has a job to do. Buy, buy, buy. The firm lives on commissions. There is always a "story". Every week in fact. Test all their recommendations. You will find most are junk. A minority are bad junk, the sort which tempts you to ring up and abuse your broker. Don't. The poor guy is only doing his job. Occasionally, very occasionally, your stockbroker comes up with something good. Keep them happy with a bit of commission. But for re-balancing, I recommend using a low commission broker. High commissions can eat into your fund.

I also subscribe to a service that notifies me if a share price in the vast galaxy of shares out there has jumped a bit. No you don't need a "reason" for the jump. Somebody knows something. It is worth checking it out. If stripped of "advice" it is a cheap service, and well worth it. It is amazing how many good and interesting shares swim into view using this service.

You will notice that throughout this book, I have not mentioned dividends and yields. There is a simple reason for this. The purpose of this investment strategy is to invest for stability. Don't invest for dividends unless you really need the income. There are a number of reasons for this.

1. Companies with high dividends are not necessarily a safe investment. Companies do not pay dividends because of the goodness of their soul. They want to attract investors. If the company pays high dividends AND has high economic rents, all well and good. They can afford to pay dividends. But if they do not have high economic rents, avoid this investment. Sooner or later these high dividends, like all good things, will come to an end. Then you will find that you have bought a dud investment.
2. Dividends are often paid out of capital, especially for firms with low economic rents. Whether or not that activity is legal or not, that breach is too often ignored.
3. Dividends, if they end up in your bank account, usually get spent. (How many investors' spouses grab the money and spend it before you think about what you are going to do with it!). Use dividend re-investment schemes if you can for your selected companies.

Conclusion

The purpose of this book was to improve your economic welfare. But not in some zero-sum way, through short-term speculation. You need to select shares of companies that will maintain their value in the long term. The way to select these companies is to select those that operate with high economic rents. Their profits will increase over time, or remain high, and given a rational share market, the share prices of these companies will increase over time, or remain high.

Use this methodology rather than invest in funds.

Now a good fund manager makes in the long term a growth in the value of the share portfolio he/she manages of around 5% per annum over the inflation rate. That is a good one. Bad ones do far worse, and indeed lose vast sums of their investors' money.

Most funds, if you look at the MorningStar reports, are run by bad or mediocre investment managers. Their returns are consistently bad, far worse than the return provided by the apocryphal monkey throwing darts at a list of shares. Some even, those funds run by banks, deliberately make a bad return by investing their clients money in their banks' deposits. So in many cases you cannot even depend on the best intentions or honesty of your fund managers. They are all overpaid, and the vast majority do not give a good return for your money.

It is far better that you did the investing yourself, if you could be nearly certain that the method you use produces better than normal returns. Then all you need worry about is the commission costs of regularly re-balancing your portfolio. (A job that you must do).

Now, I don't want to get letters from investors who used this method who tell me "Last year, after the market dropped 25 per cent, my portfolio only broke even! I should have used that charting method advised by my brother in law."

Yes, there are charting methods that do work. Without a doubt. Most don't, but a few do. But there is a downside to using the charting method. It will take up a lot of your time. All of your spare time, in fact. The charting method only works if you spend every evening at your screen checking the current charts for you entire portfolio. Your eyes will go red! Automatically generated signals? You have to re-set them every couple of days. Employing someone else to check the charts? Even the most conscientious employees have 'personal problems' from time to time, which just happen to coincide with the phases of the moon and a big loss for you. Don't I know it! No, from my bitter experience, charting is a route to madness.

No. Medium to long term investing is the only way to go. And if you are going to go down that route, you can either do a Warren Buffet, and churn through a really massive amount of accounting information to get to a single nugget, or do it the "Economic Rents" method. Churn through much less accounting information, just a few sets of data per company, and that way you have a much higher probability of striking a lot of nuggets. You will have a plethora of choice from which you can choose a high performance portfolio.

Tax. Yes, like death, it is unavoidable. Trying to evade tax is not only illegal, and tax evaders are pursued relentlessly by every government in the world, but the process of evading tax destroys your peace of mind and happiness, as you have constantly in the back of your mind, correctly, that you are being pursued and may be caught and severely punished. It's not worth it. Tax avoidance, the legal sort, is also not worth it. Going through the contortions and expense is equally soul destroying. Living abroad and away from your natural home to avoid tax is silly. Realize that you gain from the protection and welfare of your government and be happy to pay any tax charge fully to pay for that privilege. You are making a lot of money. Paying full taxes on your profits won't send you broke in most tax regimes.

So a final word. Your success in applying this technique depends on your hard work and application. However the gains you make will vastly outweigh the time and effort you put into it. You will be streets ahead of most other investors, including the big funds, which use timeworn methodology together with very expensively gained insider information of dubious value.

Finally I would like to bring the readers attention to my other book "Increasing Returns to Scale". If you use that book to set up a separate spreadsheet to impart that different set of valuable information, you can reduce the time spent on the data hunt to provide financial data for both spreadsheets as most of the data is the same in both spreadsheets. In effect you will make significant gains of scale, and you will gain major economic rents from the combined set of information.

Chapter 13

The proposed Tax on Economic Rents

This last chapter on taxing economic rents is an addendum to the purpose of the book, which is to make safe share investments using knowledge of how to calculate the size of economic rents of corporations. You can safely ignore this chapter. However for those economically inclined, it is an interesting read.

Not only business and corporate economic rents can be taxed, but also the economic rents of paid employment can be taxed. Most individuals earn economic rents on the incomes they earn. This economic rent is that component of income over and above the absolute basic wage, and accrues to the scarcity or quasi-monopoly of that person's services in the economy.

For example, a pop star or a sports star would accrue a very high economic rent, due to the high demand for that person's services. On a lesser scale, a successful doctor or lawyer would accrue a high economic rent due to high demand and restricted access to persons entering that profession. Certain trade unions manage to increase the economic rents of their members by reducing competition and restricting access to that trade or occupation. Economic rents are essentially caused by the actions of high demand for and reduced supply of persons into a particular occupation.

The development of the theory of measuring the size of economic rents came about through the development of the theory of taxation. The development of the subject of the theory of economic rents originating in Ricardo was somewhat tortuous. Economists did not jump into the subject saying "Hey, lets make money out of this!" They began looking at the social effects of economic rents, and then how to tax them.

I mentioned E Cary Brown in a previous chapter. He wrote his article to advocate something now called the "Tax on Economic Rents" on business income, also often called the "Brown Tax" or more obscurely the "Cash Flow Tax".

Economists interested in this area (such as myself) calculate that an economic rent tax (Brown Tax) will increase tax revenue from company tax in every country that applies significant company tax by at least 30% compared to the currently applied form of corporation tax. Yet at the same time company performance, economic growth and employment, even profits, will improve. Why? Because this tax will increase capital expenditure (investment) for every company to an 'optimal' level and proportion of company activity. Companies will be more efficient. They will grow faster. The present company tax discourages capital expenditure and is highly economically inefficient and reduces national growth.

A tax on economic rents is an 'ideal' tax from the economic theory point of view, because it is non-distorting. This is called being 'neutral'. Current corporation and personal taxes are highly non-neutral and distortionary, simply because the higher the tax rate, the more it reduces the business activity of the company. A Brown Tax increase does not reduce company activity even if the tax rate is increased to 99% of the economic rent!

An additional advantage is that the tax can be fitted into a 'flat' personal income tax at the same rate as the company tax. The economic rent tax on personal incomes has a structure of a high tax-free threshold with no deductions. The tax free threshold is set at a level where personal income has a zero rent component, such as a basic wage, or the income of a laborer, or at the legal minimum wage of many countries. Any income above this tax-free threshold is therefore defined as the economic rent component of earned and investment income. If this economic rent is taxed at a flat rate, it is still in practice progressive because of the existence of the tax-free threshold. However this does not prevent the tax authorities imposing an additional progressive rate of tax if they wish. Whatever the tax rate or structure, as long as this tax is only applied on the economic rent component of income, it is 'neutral' and does not affect the taxpayer's incentive to work.

Thus it is quite possible for a country to raise both business taxes and personal income taxes using an economic rent tax. A personal economic rent tax is also an 'ideal' tax because it is also non-distortionary. On the other hand sales taxes, excise taxes, trade tariffs, and taxes on goods and services are highly distortionary and harmful, reduce economic growth, and increase unemployment. For a country to be truly competitive, it must operate using only taxes on economic rents.

Many at this point and say it is "all theoretical", a Brown Tax is not possible, and lose interest. However there is a single example in the world where a Brown Tax IS operating, and has operated very successfully over twenty years. In the 1980's Australia enacted a slightly modified form of the Brown Tax on petroleum extraction rents, (Garnaut and Clunies Ross 1975) called the Petroleum Resource Rent Tax (Petroleum and Resource Rent tax 1987). This has been very successful and has operated without a hitch since. More recently in 2012 Australia tried to apply a somewhat bowdlerized version of this tax on the rest of the mining industry. But the ferocious (and costly) opposition of the mining industry nearly brought the government down!

Another tax that is a tax on economic rents, and Henry George would love this, is a land tax on urban land. Such a tax is an ideal tax for local taxation. Again in Australia (that paragon of economic virtues) such a Henry George tax does operate for local town land taxes, called 'rates', and is called the 'unimproved land value' tax. (Unimproved land value is equal to the total value of the property less the value of the building sitting upon it). It is not the purpose of this book to describe the function of this tax. Its workings are described in detail on the web. The unimproved land value tax has operated successfully in Australia for over a century. Henry George is the patron saint of Australian local government taxation practitioners.

So in conclusion, a consistent set of economic rent taxes on businesses, personal income and urban land is quite feasible. In the case of business taxes and land taxes isolated examples are currently operating very successfully. It would not be very hard to introduce a tax on personal income net of a tax-free threshold, with few or no deductions. An economy based solely on the taxation of economic rents, with no taxes on consumption, sales or commodities would be very successful and highly competitive.

Chapter 14

The Mathematical Proof

There has been very little work published on economic rents in recent times. For one of the best and most concise proofs that the Brown Tax is a tax on economic rents, I have to go back to 1975 for an article by that great economist Joseph Stiglitz, whom I shall repeat verbatim for the first part of his article on corporate income taxes, first looking at the effect of immediate write-off costs and no interest deductibility (in other words, the Brown Tax).

The following is an extract from the article Joseph E. Stiglitz (1975). (Go to References for the complete citation).

The corporate tax as a tax on profits

A tax on corporate income with immediate write-off of costs and no interest deductibility is non-distortionary and is essentially a tax on pure profits. To see this, consider and asset yielding an income stream of *R(t)* for *t ≥ 0* and costing **C**. The present discounted value of that asset before taxation is

$$\int Re^{-rt} \, dt,$$

where *r* is the rate of interest. After taxes, if the relevant rate of discount were unchanged, with immediate write-off of costs, the net return to investing in the project is

$$(1 - \tau)[\int Re^{-rt} - C],$$

where τ is the tax rate. It immediately follows that if a project was worth under-taking before, it still is: the tax is completely non-distortionary in its effect.

We need to argue now that the relevant rate of discount is unchanged. To see this, we consider a firm which is contemplating investing a dollar with a (known marginal) return in a one period project of **i**. It can borrow at the rate **r** to finance the investment. The firm is not allowed to deduct interest, but is allowed immediate write-off of the expenditure. Thus, the net cost of the project is **(1 - τ)**, while the net return is

(1 -τ)(l +i) - (1 - τ)(l +r).

Thus, the required marginal rate of return is just **i**: investment will be carried to the point where

i = r.

Thus to repeat Stiglitz "A tax on corporate income with immediate write-off of costs and no interest deductibility is non-distortionary and is essentially a tax on pure profits". What he means by "pure profits" is "economic rents". Thus, if the above, which is a Brown Tax as described in this book, is a tax on economic rents, its tax base is a measure of economic rents.

The above is a concise proof by a famous economist that the formula described in this book measures economic rents earned by a corporation.

For those who need additional proof, I suggest that you look at the textbook Boadway and Wildasin (1984) (and succeeding editions); the chapter on the Incentive Effects of Taxation, section on Corporate Taxes, pages 326 to 331. The proof is different but to the same effect – the cash flow tax is neutral and is a tax on economic rents.

Other proofs can be found by looking up 'cash flow tax' in books on public sector economics or the economics of taxation.

Lastly, Australian economists Peter Swan and Ben Smith (Australia is about the only place where research on this subject has been done recently) revised recently the formula used in this book to show that it was not quite neutral. Basically you must divide Capital Expenditure C by $(1 + i)^{n-1}$ where i is the interest rate and n is the life of the investment and reciprocal of the economic depreciation rate. This formulation slightly *increases* the calculated value of the economic rent by reducing the value of the capital expenditure deducted. Opponents of the Brown Tax should not call for this revision, as it would increase the value of the tax paid!

References

David Ricardo, 1817. *On the Principles of Political Economy and Taxation.*

E. Cary Brown, 1948, *Business-Income taxation and Investment Incentives*, in L. Metzler et al. *Income, Employment and Public Policy: Essays in Honor of Alvin H. Hansen*, W.W. Norton, New York

Henry George, 1879, *Progress and Poverty.*

John S. Morton, Rae Jean B Goodman, 2003, *The Story of Economic Rent*, Advanced Placement Economics (3rd Ed) National Council of Economic Education, p 266.

Joseph E. Stiglitz, 1975, *The Corporation Tax*, Journal of Public Economics, 5, pp 303-311.

M.T. Sumner, 1975, *Neutrality of Corporate Taxation*, Manchester School of Economics and Social Studies, vol 43, pp 353 –363

Petroleum Resource Rent Tax Act 1987 as amended (Australia). Australian Government Publishing Service, Canberra, Australia.

Robin W. Boadway and David E. Wildasin, 1984, *Public Sector Economics*, second edition, Little, Brown and Company, Boston, pp 326-331.

R. Garnaut and A. Clunies-Ross, 1975, *Uncertainty, Risk Aversion and the Taxing of Natural Resource Projects*. Economic Journal 85, June, pp 272-87

www.ingramcontent.com/pod-product-compliance
Lightning Source LLC
Chambersburg PA
CBHW051423200326
41520CB00023B/7338